GREAT BIBLE STORIES
DAVID AND GOLIATH

Adapted by Maxine Nodel   **Illustrated by Norman Nodel**

BARONET BOOKS is a registered trademark of Playmore Inc., Publishers
and Waldman Publishing Corp., New York, N.Y.

BARONET BOOKS, NEW YORK, NEW YORK
Printed in China

In the valley of Elah, two great armies faced each other, that of the Philistines and that of the Israelites, led by King Saul.

For many years and through many battles, each side stood, neither able to claim the great victory that would end the conflict.

The Philistines were idol-worshipers and bowed to many gods, but the Israelites prayed only to their Lord, whom they knew was the one true God.

The Israelites wanted the Philistines out of their land so that they could worship God in their own way.

One day, there was a great stirring in the Philistine camp.

The Israelites watched in amazement. A giant warrior, ten feet tall, clad in bronze armor and carrying an enormous spear, broke from the Philistine ranks and strode towards the Israelites.

"I am Goliath!" he thundered across the valley. "Let one of you come and fight me, if he dares. Then this war will be decided by single combat."

For two champions to fight, instead of thousands of men, would save many lives, the Israelites knew. But where would they find any one man who could stand up to this giant.

In the Israelite army there were three brothers. Their aged father, Jesse, sent their youngest brother, David, to bring them food. Young David was in camp one morning when Goliath issued his challenge.

"Who is this Philistine who dares defy the army of God?" the boy David asked. "I will fight him."

But the grown men of the camp, even David's brothers, scoffed at him. But David persisted, until his words reached King Saul himself.

"You are only a boy," said the King. "We cannot let a boy go against a giant."

But David insisted, "When I watch over my father's sheep, I rescue the lambs from any wild beast that carries them off. I know that God will give me the strength to defeat this Philistine too."

At last, the King gave in. He offered David his own armor and weapons to use against Goliath.

But the boy found the King's armor too large and heavy. "I will fight with my own weapons in my own way," he declared.

He took his slingshot, a stick, and his shepherd's bag.

As David approached the valley, he stopped at a dried-out riverbed. Stooping down, he picked up five smooth stones and put them in his bag.

Then he went forth to face Goliath.

The giant shook with laughter when he saw David.
"Is Israel so short of men they send a boy to fight me?"
Goliath mocked.

He was not only a warrior, but a poet who wrote many of the beautiful psalms in the Bible.

David was also a mighty builder. He made Jerusalem his capital city and brought it much splendor. People called Jerusalem the City of Peace. . . the city of David.